REHEARSING HOW TO LIVE

REACHING OUT TO LIFE

MAX ROYTENBERG

iUniverse, Inc.
Bloomington

Rehearsing How To Live
Reaching Out To Life

iUniverse books may be ordered through booksellers or by contacting:

iUniverse
1663 Liberty Drive
Bloomington, IN 47403
www.iuniverse.com
1-800-Authors (1-800-288-4677)

ISBN: 978-1-4759-0976-0 (sc)
ISBN: 978-1-4759-0977-7 (hc)
ISBN: 978-1-4759-0978-4 (e)

Library of Congress Control Number: 2012905884

Printed in the United States of America

iUniverse rev. date: 04/24/2012

PREFACE

I grew up in Winnipeg, Canada, one generation removed from Europe. I lived the immigrant experience, once removed. Many of the hostilities of the European environment were transplanted and were a part of my upbringing. I trained as an economist, higher education serving as my avenue of escape from what I viewed were the limitations on my prospects in my home town. Writing from a young age as a result of an early encounter with William Shakespeare, I later suppressed and sublimated the talents I had into the requirements of a business career. Working in Canada and in undeveloped areas of the world, I became a civil servant, a retail business executive, a food industry consultant, and an individual entrepreneur. These writings describe the gamut of the living and work experience, family life, the aging experience and coping with the prospect of death.

I am in my eighth decade. Describing the aging experience, my thoughts and perspectives at this stage of my life, my hope is that I may bring some elements of learning to those who may choose to read this book

These poems have been written over a period of more than fifty years. They, in part, represent my struggle to better understand the world around me. I hope that they strike responsive chords and that they represent some truths about our world with which others can identify. I hope to generate insights as well as entertain.

One great advantage of survival to an advanced age is the opportunity for a reappraisal of the panorama of life's events. Being the survivor one gets to write the history. These writings focus on some of this, the benefits of hindsight, second guessing and maybe a few lies about what really happened. There might even be the opportunity to learn from past mistakes and misjudgments. Perhaps we can review events without the attendant emotion that may have clouded our judgment at the particular time. The reader may find this as useful as I did.

These writings draw conclusions about life and its events that may offer a useful perspective on relationships, attitudes to life, the world around us, parents and children, ageing and death. Our society has changed with time and is undergoing change at an increasingly rapid pace. How have we dealt with these elements of life in our society, what have we done right or wrong, what we might have done, what we might still do? These questions are the subject matter of this book.

Life is a rehearsal every day for how we may face tomorrow better prepared.

MMR

ACKNOWLEDGEMENTS

I would like to acknowledge the role my wife, Miryom, has played in permitting me to construct the new life that has made these writings possible. My Muse, Miryom has given me permission to be the selfish artist that the devotion required to produce these writings demanded. Hers were the many and long hours spent essentially alone while my mind ranged the pathways of memory and thought. Her appreciation and enthusiasm for the messages I have to share encouraged me to persist. I cannot thank her enough for believing I had something worthwhile to share.

I would like to acknowledge the contributions of all my children, David, Deborah, Judi and Daniel, with their partners and children, the grandchildren they have blessed me with, they have instructed me as to the true rewards of our presence in this current existence.

I acknowledge my undying gratitude to the Life-force that governs everything we are and blessed me the gift of my life partner, lost and found again, to yield a life renewed.

Further acknowledgment must also be made for all those unnamed souls who have peopled my world, and provided the grist for my egotistical mill, the raw material of these offerings. I acknowledge and thank the many unknown individuals who made this volume physically possible.

Pouligny-Montrachet, France, July, 2011

DEDICATION

This work is dedicated to Miryom, who, in spite of over fifty years of distracted inattention, had constant love on offer when I came calling, bold and brave enough, at last, to assault the proud tower. My Muse, she has liberated me, gifting me with the power and the strength to pen these offerings. She is the sweet "Cookie" of the High Tea of my life.

MMR, November, 2011 Arizona

Contents

I
<u>Looking Back</u>

II
<u>People I've Learned From</u>

III
<u>Milestones</u>

IV
<u>Looking Ahead</u>

V
<u>Coming To Terms</u>

I

∽

LOOKING BACK

REHEARSING HOW TO LIVE

Here I sit and contemplate the unfolding universe,
imagine worlds are mere grains of sand in an unseen titan's
    purse,
consider that my rages are both pointless and perverse,
consider all my loved ones and how to living-life rehearse.
See the brilliant light of an ivory moon shining almost full,
invisible forces round the world the rushing tides do pull,
invisible forces round the world untold emotions pour,
leading people many times to thoughtless actions we abhor.
The raging sun conditions many populations near and far
to somehow organize their lives differently and to not aspire
as urgently as those where the climates are much more
    moderate.

We can see how seriously our place of living does our fates
    dictate,
how often we're the idle objects of forces beyond our ken,
dreamlike, we believe we're the sole masters of our Why
    and When.
Perhaps those thinkers we know well of distant eastern bent
who preach acceptance come closer to the world's hid intent.
Shakespeare told us we are brief players on a stage,
each presenting once only a unique presence on Life's page-
who we are and what we are indelibly recorded for all
    human time-
perhaps we need rehearsals as we struggle to perfect the
    rhyme.

I see my living past consumed with rages and discontent,
with fierce urgings to greatly alter fate and to actively
   dissent,
measuring my success and satisfactions with how radically I
   rent
the fabric of brute reality that fate did to me present.

Now I am more willing to surrender and accept the sweep
   of fate.
I discern more clearly what I face, the scale of forces
   inchoate,
I, no longer, being more realistic, my feebleness berate
as advancing age and diminished capacities seem it to me
   dictate.

Now and then to the barricades once again I race
as some issue I can't tolerate stares me squarely in the face.
A new-found strength and swelling rage does quicken me
   my pace
and I set forth determinedly to all obstacles erase.

Yet, these days I mostly contemplate the unfolding universe.
Perhaps worlds are grains of sand in some unseen titan's
   purse.
I polish my performance and perfect my rhyming verse.
I focus on my loved ones and my living-life rehearse.

LOOKING BACK

The years have flown by and now I am too old to try.
How could I let them fly so idly by?
Which was correct, that selected or that cast aside,
those issues not then chosen in my preening pride?
Reviewing these grave matters with perspective
without all the immediacy of urgency's incentive,
shrinks these choices of their imperious scale,
raising questions of their import as their urgencies do pale.

Shall we now rethink it all-the old intents-
pick again at ancient heal-ed sores-
crawl through all the hoary arguments
thinking now to settle the old scores?

Let it rest now, let it rest.
We did all the things then as we could then best.

CAN WE SEE?

Skitter-scatter, wind-swept droplets beat staccato
rhythms on our glassy apertures
shattering into filigree the apparitions that
dance so visibly in the light of rainless day.

Looking back at our histories, our views clouded
by the torrents of emotion, silvering shadows
gilding the realities, we shield the constructs
that protect our private images of the past.

Do we ever truly see our histories clearly in the light?

WALL STREET BLUES

Is this picture really true?
Did I squander what I promised you
for vain hope of dreamed-of gain-
treasure lost, I feel the pain.
This is not a story new,
my having seen before this dismal view,
constantly welcoming the future's golden lure,
I often built a financial sepulcher
anew to test my living's strength,
to recover wealth for us at length.

There yet remains some living time.
We know not when breathing's rhyme
will be halted and brush aside
all fervent promises we confide.

Shall we yet learn--can it be tried?
With what we have, be satisfied?

FOR A WHILE

We sit and gaze at the evening sky,
a silvered moon to catch our eye,
we touch and kiss, heedless of an inner cry
that weeps at time lost, time gone by.

We relish the reborn day that we have found-
pushing back the silent sound
of rushing time-the flow so onward bound
toward the end in which all life is drowned.

The joy of having you so near,
the sight of you, my joy is clear
in the smile we share when you appear-
I touch your skin like gossamer.

Our passions rising from our need
to find at last, in word, in deed,
in thought, in hope, in shar-ed creed,
the things we are-instantly freed.

We fiercely seize on this new dawn
and dream that life goes on and on
as failing powers cast doubt upon
the doings we are wishing done/undone.

Brave spirits urge us-go, seek the trial !
Go forward! Take your courage. Smile!
The road's before you, many a mile,
though it be, we fear, just for a while.

We rage, we curse, we shed some blood,
our joys new-found to be denied?
Our miracle shattered-in the mud?
This gift from God, so soon defied?

We gather strength and courage-smile-
we hold each other tightly, meet the trial,
cherish our treasures yet a mile,
blessings gifted yet a while.

WHAT'S THE SCORE?

It's strange to think about the past so many years gone by
and suddenly see I'm old my body, it did watch them fly.
What makes my blood run cold, athinking long on this,
seems just yesterday I wore short pants, shooting marbles so
    they'd kiss.
Such long shots were my greatest chance, so I'd at last be
    the best,
show my mettle, beat my friends, above all be better than
    the rest.

Impending deaths, they concentrate the mind, peeking
    round the curve of liquid time,
unsought, unknown and coming when? Coming swift or
    slow, with pains to climb?

Are you the enemy or blessed friend?
Is there more, or here on earth it ends?
Do we dream it all to soften unknown fears,
Are we piling prayers, to economize on tears,
each human sends on many mystic altars,
seeking a redemption somewhere in the stars.
Or is there a Life-force which all this mystery blends?
A place where a soul can find the eternity it spends?

Life's myriad joys of untold various range,
so carelessly we add each precious day
and spend them thoughtlessly, loose change,
from our meager store, our treasured life array.
Little thought we give as through life we range
was there merit for the coin we spent?
Did we well, if later on we contemplate,

no serious cause to regret, foment dissent
with judgments then? Now, it's very late.
Whatever the outcome, this is now our fate.

WRITINGS ON THE WALL

I sit me down, machine at hand, to write me down a list
of all the records in my past, filed, stored and then
   dismissed.
I kept it all, my precious words, from youth to ancient age,
aside they were placed with patient toil, carefully spaced
   there on each page.

Now here I sit, six decades hence, no single sentence to be seen
of the words I stored so carefully my posterity to screen.
How can it be that I am here, no evidence I toiled,
that I was there, fought for my place and vigorously roiled
smooth waters to force judgment, my own true print,
when in my view those presented, had for me insufficient hint
of the matters' most essential need.
that I strived to ensure given proper heed.

The early works were left secure at home
when I first began the world to roam
and carelessly left them there in trust
with little thought that with time they must
be discarded with the trash as the custodians, falling away,
did their own memoirs ultimately betray.

Then the records of those student years,
challenges of mind and the future's fears,
the new-found skills, economist proud,
mounting higher, declaiming to the crowd,
advising power and policy deduced
how income for them was to be produced.
All the records of the many trials
faced by farmers, there in my files.

What did I see there?
What did I write recorded there
for second memory's sight
when I examine them in fullest light?
What of my thoughts and insights clear,
attending a food merchant seer.
Of market mysteries, cut and thrust,
make a fortune or go bust,
selling foods and fads and flooring wax,
meats and beans and add the tax.
Victories and schemes of gain,
five year plans to profits attain.

Jealously I in my papers placed
attainments which blind time erased.
Much was lost, a pittance saved,
as the wife and house, in past so craved,
departed from my hand and view-
I away for a life anew.

Begin again a chapter bold,
leaping blind-the blood runs cold-
translating bookish untried plans
into realities, world-bridging spans,
systems spread across a nation and the globe,
sturdily resisting fierce markets' probe,
curbing wills and malicious hands
to build a house that yet still stands.

The schemes I spun, the words I wrote,
the arguments, unbidden, from my throat,
records, files, submissions without end,
with weighty words the shelves did bend.

My creations were everywhere piled-
my living space with files were tiled.
But for a new bride-her needs I must meet
there must be a space to place her feet.
With fortune's grace we found a place
ample for living and for storage space.
With time passing, new challenges arise
work feeding on my words-no surprise.
Again the written word on every side
as I traveled the world and, filled with pride,
proposed solutions for peoples' problems grave
on every side, millions here were poverty's slave.

Too soon this kind of work it palls.
Too often on arid ground it falls.
No matter what we try and hard,
the vessel breaks and we but see the shard.
It is even painful to relate,
piled reports did no gains create.
We must go on and seek some worthwhile place,
find work of interest to fill our mental space.

Soon enough we respond to the supermarket's lure,
become an advocate the problems there to cure.
Speeches, hearings and improvements to advertise,
add to records, better methods quickly to devise.
Meetings, speakers, great conferences to organize,
compendiums, volumes gathered and offered to the wise.
Satisfying work, leaving traces in the sand,
contributions repaying gifts I had from my native land.

Over then and I return to my home
to a caregiver be, sometime the world to roam.

Contemplate, almost three decades racing past-
Why did our love all through the years not last?
I, so busy seeking worth from love and life,
failed to see the love lost from my wife.
Then comes death-murdering life with ugly feet-
carrying sorrow and major changes in life to greet.

House too big-painful sights assail on every side-
escape my past to elsewhere find more hopeful tides to ride.
Facing then the records of my past,
evidence on paper of things that I did last,
tome on tome created from my mind.
Suddenly it seemed to me that I'd been blind.
What worth this product, for whom should it be retained?
I would not be there. Who could have it for them explained?

The worth of work was always on the ground,
work's value there is no longer to be found.
Who would value these tomes when I am gone?
Burdens for my offspring all that would be won.

What of the product that never produced a gain
but paid me well for helpless subject's pain?
It eats my soul like acid that I failed-
I did not overcome the obstacles-the barriers were not
      scaled.
What interest for my children could be there?
What need to store it in some space I could not spare?

Anger boils for all the wanted things undone-
aspirations to perfection-goals I never won.
Wipe the proof away that I could not have it all-
destroy the evidence-now it is dispersed beyond recall.

The ego trip is gone, I alone can tell the tale,
see at last reality-what is the Holy Grail?
The children who had less of me
because I toiled to prove I'd be making marks the world
    would see?
Leaving my track on world history?
I might have made a difference, spouse deprived of nurture's
    care
where she lacked that warm hand that I could not spare
because I was so focused on goals written in the air?

I, now, most fortunate of men,
to live to weigh the chosen roles again-
see children's smiles-and loving kisses too-
in spite of errors now I so sadly rue.
Those records I dismissed from human sight
that felt my anger, they woke me to the light.
Now it filters unbidden into my secret hidden brain,
carrying with it, like an acid bite, regret's new-found pain,
sudden now, I see it graven, I see it written all,
now I see my past and future written on the wall.

I SING MYSELF TO SLEEP

Staring into the darkness of my slumber time, there is no
    rhyme.
I can read the years that silvered the hair upon my head.
At my leisure, aided by the light of memory, I can dissect
the body of evidence stored haphazardly, lancing cruelly
to the heart of all the matters I placed there to put off the pain
for another day. It will be some time before I sleep tonight.
Imprisoned in my mind's cage, Youtube-like visions-clips
play over and over again on my inner screen, running-
    revealing-
the scenes of my story which I would like my playwright to
    re-write.

On seeking your repose, is this new song you wish to sing
    the thing?
Why did we not rehearse the songs we wished in tune to sing?
Why must we rehearse our roles solely in retrospect?
We know how we would sing them now-if only we could
    them correct,
if only we could-could get the chance to sing those songs
    again.
Now the tune's in harmony, now-now it is not like it was then,
Now with our new perspective, the lyric is well rhymed.
We polish and perform it, singing tunefully in our dream time.
As author and composer, director of the play-regret our goad-
we're now really ready to take this show on the revival road.
The trouble is that our theater has long vanished in past times,
many of the other actors now departed for other unknown
    climes.

I cannot help but sing these songs to the subjects in my
    dreams.
Though they are gone maybe I can retain the tune that to
    me now seems
so much sweeter-sweeter tunes for other valued actors in my
    life still,
I am eager to sing them the newer lyrics with the best of will,
sing to them those rhymes I learned to sing during my
    sleeping times
when after years of practice I discerned the essence of my
    crimes.

II

PEOPLE I'VE
LEARNED FROM

TEACHERS

The man I am is made of parts, pieces from many places.
We all start from that mysterious mix, origins with traces
from an alchemy we little know how came it to the fore,
contributions centuries ago slyly placed for us in store.
The man or woman we will be is also shaped by those we
    know,
those persons we encountered from whom our ideas flow.

They may not know they're teaching us,
no formal lecture or a passing word discuss,
they yet teach us lessons impressed upon on our minds,
stored messages sometimes of the strangest kinds.

We learn from parents, teachers, our closest friends,
the time of learning lessons really never ends,
a chance encounter in the street,
a scene unbidden our eyes greet,
a book we choose to look at closely,
a program on TV to which we listen mostly-

our lives are shaped in ways we cannot calculate,
we are often creatures forged by random blinded fate,
we are works in progress every day that we're alive,
taught to be the What we are that directs what does us
    drive.

ANOTHER YEAR WINDS DOWN

I'm seeing numbers now-the new millennium-that I
    thought I'd never see.
I hear tales of companions gone, chums, with whom we did
    our sums
Over many hours, in our youth, happily carefree.
We had no thought of marching time
now writ so legibly on thin and papery skin,
just living's games and happy rhyme
as we made our way together through thick and painful thin.

Now, gratefully, with careful tread,
we seek a warming sun
to coddle us-with buttered bread-
we sing aloud, all seeking fun-
attending now the birthing year, alas, with dread,
a little living yet to run.

WHAT NOW?

Life is pleasant with a lover by your side,
it matters not old age, taken now in stride,
we heat our bones in the sunny warmth of remembered Whiles
we shared, our minds are sound and we yet retain our
    rueful smiles,
treasuring now our bonded life here resurrected from our past,
knowing, tasking mind and spirit, resisting time until the
    very last.
We pleasure in the touch, the sight of each day that does appear-
but what of our losses cascading, the Tomorrows we yet fear?
Like shadows in our mind, our future prospects haunt our
    Nows
as we behold the fates of fellows that we pass with furrowed
    brows.
Strive as we may to cast these thoughts behind
they prey like phantoms attendant on our minds,

We thought we were constructed well, made of sterner stuff,
living life day by day with joys that more than yield enough,
yet the specter, all unsought, it stalks our waking thoughts
draining pleasure with the speculation of potential Future's
    lots.
Will illness linger on or mounting pain our joys destroy?
Will our minds fail us-neither past nor present to deploy?
We resolve-considered thought-when the time has come to
    face the test
that, sole together, above all, will we seek the means to find
    our rest.
Now at last we've found our path to peace-
jointly, only, will we retain the lease.

WANING DAYS?

Have I *changed?*
The issues and the questions that once sent me
to the barricades, guns bristling,
now just yield fatigue, bone-weary fatigue.
Laziness or lassitude?
Am I winding down?
Are these my waning days?
Shall I gird my loins for battle
against unceasing waves of evil
I must personally confront?

Those tasks, I know,
must surely be performed
by whom, if not I?

My friend, he died.
He left vast empty spaces
that can never be filled.
Or can they?
Will they be filled in some form
"undreamed of in your philosophies, Horatio*"?

This then is the way of the world,
the natural course of human events,
failing hands, will it or not,
must pass on all their tasks.
Are these my waning days?
Or, does there remain
some "spit and vinegar"
to "spice up" my latter times.

*<u>Hamlet,</u> William Shakespeare

AN OPEN BOOK

We live our lives with parts in hidden places,
we all have secrets filling in the darkened spaces,
thoughts we keep hidden from whomever he who delves,
sometimes there are whispers we keep hidden even from
    ourselves.
There are things we would not ever tell a soul,
actions taken-afterwards we deeply despise our role-
feelings, if but revealed would fully compromise our soul
or agitate the party for whose generous good will we troll.

It's sometime hard to keep it quiet-it percolates inside-
we bite our lips, store all away, find places all to hide.
There's some we share, some we can bury, O so very deep!
Some we visit rarely in our waking thoughts or even in our
    sleep.

These things they take their toll-they weigh on us, these
    kernels in our mind,
the energies they exercise banish the peace we seek to find.
We understand the blessings the confessional does bring
to tortured minds, washing out thoughts that round the
    mind do ring.

How grateful I am today that with you my mind's an open
    book.
You know my thoughts, in every cranny, in every hidden
    nook.
I may seem simple now, no more mysteries to hide,
you know it all, feel free to all my many weaknesses deride,

now I risk it all for better or for worse,
for love, affection, or even, horrors! An everlasting curse.
Familiarity, they say, contempt does bring in tow,
though I know it's hard and it is true, I will risk it even so.

There is no peace like this beside nature's burbling brook,
better than the peace that comes, O lucky one, when life's
    an open book.

REALITY CHECK

The time has come and past, the years are three score and ten.
We've paid them scant attention as our times went rushing by.
The children are now well grown with thoughts beyond our
    ken,
sweet offspring here in sufficient number to immortality imply.

We must give consideration to our end of time, of when it
    comes,
no one, yet, that we know of gets out this living life alive.
Counting on our fingers, it is evident that we must do our
    sums,
we must elaborate it clearly, our desired ends' elements
    contrive.

With passing years we've attended such occasions-somber, sad.
Perhaps, with reason, persons passing on, sadly, much too
    soon.
For myself, it's not for me-I see too many reasons to be glad.
Why keep on singing if, clearly, we are no longer carrying
    on the tune.

It gives us joy to see our children, living, flourishing, so well,
we may not see it now but with passing years' perspective it
    will all be clear.
We might have done more and we have much, much, more
    to tell-
but that's our fate, it must be said, no matter how many
    years we're here.

We have plumbed our weaknesses and tested, some, our
    strengths,
traveled some around the globe-there's always more to see,
saw beauty in its many forms, struggled, strived and gone to
    serious lengths,
felt passion, rage, consuming fear and-fortunate-found a
    love to set us free.

Now let us speak of children and the hope, some kernels
    left behind-
close to them, in their growing, like a warm hand in glove
climbing up the slope, in their collection plate they'll find,
comfort, knowledge, insight, enough needed love,
we've left some generous blend as through their lives they
    bravely wend.

Now speak of love, perhaps carried hidden through many
    a long year, nurtured in your secret places, your chance
    missed through youthful fear,
struggling over decades to "make a silk purse from a sow's ear",
if fortunate, arrived finally, at last, beside you there, near,
    warm and dear.

We must come to terms, we can't have it all the way that we
    would will,
though it's far from clear to us for whom will fall the task
we must trust that time will furnish one to further tend the
    mill
and grind out the solutions-questions we know not the How
    to ask.

So, let parting time a celebration be, drink one-two or even
  three,
for me play Beethoven, Joni Mitchell, Leonard Cohen-Bob
  Dylan's twang,
Bocelli, Streisand-the many whom I loved, their message,
  when they sang,
and their melodies which so often did my children sing-
joy uncontained, whenever for me they made the rafters ring.

We count among them the wider brood whom we have
  grown to love,
the grandkids, who give such joy, and into our lives were
  interwove
as we briefly touched their lives, leaving happily some useful
  thoughts
that they may take and look at, some, placed in their
  treasure trove,
wherever their passion drives them, whatever their final lots,
we leave this message for them, we are lining up the dots.

This testament is for our survivors, may they long survive
  our time,
We leave it here in crystal-clearest verse for everyone to see,
adorned, as usual-an egotist-in my simplistic and most
  imperfect rhyme,
for when our transition times have come and we at last are free.

III

MILESTONES

A Diamond Jubilee

A diamond jubilee.
As time rushes on
I stand awe-struck at my survival.
I breathe in and out, walk about,
striving for better things.

I worship at the feet of my miracle bride
bringing me daily gifts of love, understanding and care,
unseen since crouching at my mother's knee.

I am conscious of the passage of time to this time.
I am conscious of the rarity of the gift in my hands.

Look around you!
Do you see the fortune strewn at your feet?
Do you enjoy the jewels in your life-
Do you enjoy your Nows?
Why wait as I did to celebrate a jubilee?

SEVENTY-FIFTH BIRTHDAY

I come before you, eyes wide with great surprise.
I come before you wearing
my age seventy-five disguise.
Long ago I decided I would not age
beyond the year I'm thirty-five.
I would keep it steady there at that age
as long as I'm alive.

My children have grown past me,
going about their chores,
each day I grow more youthful,
my behavior everyone deplores.
I splash in every puddle,
my hair's hung to my waist,
my affairs are in a muddle,
my clothes are in real bad taste,
I sing my songs in public
without warning or restraint,
when I stand up in a public place
my children start to faint.

What fun it is to be an age
when we don't give a damn.
This is where in life we're at,
there is no place for sham.
We're happy here to greet the world,
come with us and celebrate,
an own true love, family, friends,
joy unbounded we create.

Here's to us, let's toast to life
and enjoy this moment now,
let us live our lives, savor well each day
the best way that we know how!

WONDERSTRUCK

Miraculous!
To live this life at water's edge,
the thronging crowd, some pledge, or thought?
Pursuing what?
We seek for places to make our mark,
to fill more than space, to add to life's spark.
Now, look at the shadows gathering round.
What do we leave?
Small wisdom, found?

Take the time now to contemplate the scene.
Sweat from your fevered brow
has moistened, made pastures green-
have you left a trace of life
to rival what you cast askance?
The length of twist and turn and strife,
making up your living's dance,
cause you wonder at the world you missed,
that in your rushing passed you by.
That perfect bloom, that spreading tree,
the clouds' panorama in the sky,
that child's perfection-so beautiful-
that you before you see,
not to mention all the shining souls-miraculous-
that sprang from what you be.

Majestic futures in great surplus-gifted-are the reason that
    we be.
With luck we do remain, our hearts are full, we are in ecstasy,
grand,... replete,... at the infinite universes contained in we.

BLOSSOMS IN THE SNOW

Will our waning days of living
leave some blossoms in the snow?
Is there a residue of reason worth preserving?
Is there a message for our children,
hints for our inheritors-
do we have something left to say?

I live each day in pleasant monotony after a frenetic life,
never enough time to do all I wished to do.
I now have the pleasure of filling my life
with inconsequentialities,
with simple amusements.

I share my life with the woman of my dreams,
the unrequited dream of my youth realized at last.
What more precious gift can living grant,
surviving to realize such a dream?

My children live life around me-
how fortunate I am!
My grandchildren, acquiring the tools they need-
constructing new lives;
my essence lives on in miraculous new shapes,
creating new worlds.
My siblings yet live on with me;
my parents built well, unwittingly,
with their blind struggles to survive,
with their gifts of love and DNA,
creating what we are and transmit.

I scribble a rhyme,
I let the clay speak to me
until the images emerge.
I've left traces in my past,
changing lives for the better-
hopefully for the better.
I may yet with a word or act-
the climate, hot or cold-
I may yet leave some blossoms
from my winter's time.

I READ A BOOK TODAY

I read a book today.
I saw myself mirrored in the inventions of another mind.
Not surprising.
We can often find the things we are contemplating
expressed in other people's work.
But, seeing this-seeing the journey made by another man,
one who has gone further on the path I am traveling-
I see more clearly where I am going
and where I have come from.
I see I need no longer be ashamed to teach, or preach.
My young are more inclined to listen
if they see I face imminent death.
They would listen more then, perhaps.

I am dying, as we all are from the first day of our birth.
Most of us do not know the date of our death.
Surely, we would live better lives
if we led them as if today's day was our last.
We would take the time to pay close attention
when a loved one spoke.
We would then spend less time
planning for the tomorrow that may never come,
valuing the things that are things rather than people.

I have the good fortune to have survived
to contemplate my death,
to tell my story,
to tell my children I love them,
have always loved them and, if possible,
have loved my grandchildren even more.
I have survived to tell my lover, my bride, that I love her

and have loved her all the adult years of my life.
I want to tell all my family
and my friends I love them.
I glory in all the people in my life.
I love life,
I love the beautiful world we live in,
with all its stains and blemishes.

I read a book today. I learned something
I learned it is not too late to say these things
and not too soon.

LIVING IT UP, AGAIN!

Seven decades cross the tidal bar
waves wearing away the stone,
marking lines on faces, like a scar,
wear and tear on every bone.
Yet, life has sweetened every day,
eyes that shine with dreamed of love,
days like those of youth renewed, display
an ardor and needs matched like a hand in glove
that I thought had gone away.
Living it up again, my friends, living it up again!

There's many a tale along the way,
pain like syrup slowly flowed
across the years, golden dreams were turned to clay
in spite of many of living's gifts bestowed,
passions found and too soon lost,
hopes nourished, thoughts lost beyond repair,
add up the years and count the cost.
Enough! My lesson now I do declare,
Living it up again, my friends, living it up again!

There are lessons here for all to see,
life's answered riddle here I can unveil-
smile, strive ever and always to be free,
dare to love, take the risk you fail.
Make children to yield joys untold,
seek work that will your heart fulfill,
you will witness as does your life unfold,
such joyous times-shout out, be loud and shrill!
Living it up, again. my friends, living it up again!

Living it up, again, my friends, living it up again!

MULTI-LAYERED CAKE

Have you seen my life?
Is this the fate of everyone?
There are some without a wife,
some without their children done,
some who have their lives cut clean,
some who do the heights attain.
Some with lives that are evil, mean,
whose doings leave in life a stain,
some content to pass the time
seeking simple pleasures, simple rhyme.

Others rush to grapple, climb,
as if for life to extend the lease.
Some put at risk their life and limb
looking not for peace,
seeking a life of great adventure,
others risk a life of censure,
taking chances, sink or swim.

There are those must lead the pack-
can't tolerate the line-
greedy, hungry, they crave the highest track,
from birth to death, their sole incline.

Others seek but to give aid
to companions all along the way,
seeing this the only way to live,
or devote their life entire to pray.

These constructions I now contemplate,
each soul can their life remake,
totting up their living's slate,
lives can be a many-layered cake.

I did not do one simple thing,
my life it rang-ed far and wide,
earning both pain and joy's bell to ring,
venturing great risks on living's tide.

Gave aid to some, grasped for my own,
sought leadership and place of pride,
pursued ambition until t'was flown,
held on tight enjoying the rocky ride.

I lived enough to many hungers slake,
I lived my life akin a multi-layered cake.

FORGIVENESS

I work the clay. It is soft and smooth in my hands,
my fingers shape it at my will until the image in the clay
leaps into my mind, taking on a life of its own.

It is just the beginning-this work may be far different
in the end-larger, smaller, rough or smooth,
beautifully curved or crude.
I may let it dry or keep it moist-working, working it-
until it speaks to me, ***enough***

Or I may grow weary, tire… grow impatient!
Distracted, I may turn to other things, let it harden… dry.
The clay forgives me all my sins. If it breaks, I may repair it,
smoothing over all the wounds, reshape by grinding away,
or re-moisten, renew, re-shape the image,

The life you have created-you are yet alive-what of the images
you have left behind? What of the lives you've touched
that yet remain behind? Can you repair? Renew? Re-moisten?
Re-build another image?
Refresh? Reshape? Remove the flaws you see?
Are you too weary to seek forgiveness?

LIFESCAN

I am looking down at my life
from the height of many years-
approaching a half-century, almost a century-
You can too!

What do you see happening
across those years?
What has happened?
Take the time to study it.
You have the life to study it.
You have all of your life to study it.

Can you see a pattern?
Can you make sense of your kaleidoscope?
Zoom in on the satellite map,
find the cancers in the MRI of your life?

Where did I go wrong? Where did I go right?
Where did you go right or wrong?
Where did you too soon abandon the field?
Where did you persist and grow skilled-
halting steps that grew to strides
crowned with achievement?

Fear and self-loathing morphing
into confidence and forgiveness;
anger and disgust, impatience
and discontent that evolved,
evolved slowly. O! Too slowly-
into patience and understanding;
people-crosser to people-minder

satisfying needs to get your way;
clumsy, hurried word-smith, error-prone,
morphing into unconscious access
to vast treasuries of "le mot juste"

Could this be your story?

There is more, even more that we cannot talk about,
that you know but will not talk about;
things that stir the beat of pulse.

If we can make some sense of it all
can such knowledge be transmitted?
Transmuted?
Can it be shared or gifted?
Can you/we learn from it?

Will students find their way to the mountaintop-
Your/our mountaintop-my mountaintop-to seek our
    knowledge?
Could they-will they-unlike us, study and revise earlier as
    they go?

Can we learn from it? Can we change our ways?
Can we undo what we should not have done?
Should we?
Shall we?

IV

∼

LOOKING AHEAD

HAPPY SONG

Wrap your arms around me and
hug me to your heart.
The sun is shining brightly,
now say we'll never part!

So rare to sing a happy song and
sing it right out loud.
Swing me round again, my love,
we'll join the dancing crowd!

Ask me now no questions
and I'll tell you no more lies.
Let's trip the light fantastic and
admire endless starry skies.

There's pain enough to go around–
better keep it hid inside–
it's rare to find a friend so close
in whom we feel we can confide.

Think happy thoughts of birds in spring,
of flowers preparing for a summer fling,
We'll walk and talk and buy some teddy bears,
sing happy songs and vanish all our cares.

Let's dream a life that has no death,
sweet smells around like baby's breath,
we know our lives have pain to spare,
for just today let's leave it there.

Wrap your arms around me,
hug me to your heart,
the sun is shining brightly,
say now we'll never part.

STEPPING STONE

I was walking on my way
and tripped,
catching my foot
on a raised crack in the pavement.
I fell….heavily-
I am too heavy-
I am too old to be agile.

Embracing a bloody scrape,
tomorrow's bluish bruise,
tomorrow's random ache
of my own making.
I rise…slowly,
brush myself off,
embarrassed,
as strangers-older, mainly-
my companions in time
on this rotation,
gather round a fallen comrade.

"Oh yes, I'm fine," I say-
"stupid of me-
not looking where I was going!
Thank you. Yes, fine, just fine!"

I slink off,
back to my anonymity.
I nurse new reminders
of the path that lies ahead.

TOUCHING HANDS

Let me capture here these sweet syrup moments
in my kaleidoscopic time,
having trod the boards now more years
than the fabled three score and ten, in my rhyme
share-bristling pride and secret fears-
the wonders I beheld-behold-
my young, their pursuit of life untold.

Then, speak to me of all your special child in life has done
to swell your heart, to fulfill all the secret dreams you'd spun.
If your tale wants patient telling and explaining, painfully seen,
I comprehend harsh circumstance, the price of life's careen
that has stunted all their brightest futures. O! So rightly theirs!
It made your passing here, so unjustly, full of pain and cares.

As for myself, I can scarce contain my surging joy,
restrained but barely-ancestral memory-for fear of the evil eye,
it is difficult to show reserve, to be deliberately coy-
I revel in my good fortune-my children's large appetite to try.
Perhaps the secret lies in how we so differently view the world.
For me the thrill, their flags, so varied, are courageously
    unfurled.

There is no life lacks losses and experiences of pain,
the missteps are the condiments flavoring life's meal,
learning yields the produce when drought's replaced by rain,
as long as health remains life's passing wounds to heal.
Reach out our hands to touch our offspring-
patient always, there the parent stands-
watching hopefully their strivings
to meet living's harsh unlimited demands.

SHARING TALES

So, we've come here to share some stories
of our living time.
We are just like most of the guys on the block,
but surviving longer.

It's true the young ones are in a different place,
a place we can't even imagine.
How did it happen that the times we thought so fast
now look like we were standing still?
They make us feel like we were cave-dwellers.

It feels good to be surrounded by those
with whom we can share memories
of times when we were the actors
on the stage we imagined
was the main attraction of the show.

Remember the year of the Great Snow-
we dug caves, the snow walls sparkling like diamonds
in the morning light piercing the northern dark
of our working days being born.
We had to free ourselves from the frigid cocoons
woven by the weather each night at our front doors.

Remember the Great Flood-
we didn't go to school for a week-
working on the dikes, the free coffee and sandwiches,
being driven by City vehicles to the cityscapes
turned to lakefront in the usually arid prairie-
boating like admirals along city streets,
filling and slinging bags of sand-

we were heroes.
It was hard to go back to being ordinary.

How about the Great Blackout?
Captive in our darkened homes
with the flickering light of fireplaces,
for night light and heat,
waiting for the return of power.
We imagined heroic roles for ourselves,
abandoned cave-dwellers surviving the unknown
on subsistence rations.

Remember the beauty of our ice-clad trees
shimmering in the starlight,
offering up their shattered branches
in mute supplication
under the burden of the silvered frozen rain
when the new day exposed their pain.

Tracing the fates of old friends,
good fortune and bad fortune-
who married well and who did not,
whose body failed and whose body did not-
weren't we the lucky ones?

Who soared to the heights of public acclaim
and who vanished almost without a trace?
Whatever happened to Jack and Jill?
I can't believe that Joe is still alive-
wasn't he the sickly one?
Who would have believed that Bill would do so well?
Look at Marge! Now a jet-setter surviving all
her husbands with a rich divorce.

They sure didn't look like they had the stuff
when they were in school with us.
How about John?
He did well-we always knew he would.

So, how many grandchildren do you have?
Where are you going this winter?

We huddle round, our shuddering shoulders
warming each the other with memories of our past,
peering dimly into the Future's mists
beginning to cloud our eyes.
Looking back we now perceive
the rising heights of living's path that in that early instant
betrayed little of their incline,
that now appears momentous
in the categories of our times.

The tales we now tell of those far distant times
are showered with a gloss-gildings
that erase fissures and imperfections
flavoring these events in our minds
with satisfactions and accomplishments
we are more than eager to widely share-
mantling ourselves with a little majesty.

We permit ourselves elaborations with each telling
that reinforce our belief in the rhyme of our historical facts.

We were giants grappling with dark forces
that threatened the very essence of our lives-
our futures, the futures of our children and our wives,
evil purposes we blunted with our unique resources.

Now we look forward to our golden years
with general applause ringing in our ears.

We are full of fury and of sound-
let the little children gather round-
we are founts of wisdom and all confound.
Our offspring smile at what's in store,
a new-born hero has been found-
they have heard it all before,
a version sparer and more finely ground.

This is our new role-hear the story curled-
we present images that so much redound
with ambitions to repair the world-
tales for a new generation crowned,
all our ambitions' flags, full unfurled.
Hear of our accomplishments even more renowned!

We promote visions-challenge impending strife-
of what our young should do in life.

Let not, dear children, fate your train derail.
Recount for us all of it in full detail!

We are looking ahead!

SUNSHINE AND CLOUDS

I live on an island in the Atlantic Ocean.
They call some of the water
around here the Irish Sea-
let's not kid ourselves-
this is the Atlantic Ocean.

There is lots of water around,
and there is lots of rain around.
This place is green from all the water.
The water goes into the sky
leaving all the salt behind,
and comes down all fresh and sweet,
a lot of it like mist.

It tickles my skin-
I love the feel of it,
it makes the air soft and soggy,
it lends an impressionist air to all I see,
softening the edges of my reality.

Sometimes it really pours,
and the water, the dampness
and the chill, make my aged bones ache
so I am really miserable
and its hard to be my chirpy self.

Yes, it is cloudy a lot of the time,
but the sun fights the good fight.
I awake to a gloomy morning-
dampening my spirits,

-I come from a sunny country-
but the sun fights and fights,
and by golly we have a beautiful sunny day
and all's right with the world.
Those days that I wake
to a surprise-
the sun in my eyes-
well, that's just brilliant!

This is the life we looked forward to.

A VIEW TO THE FUTURE

Look at the horizon stretching as to infinity.
A sun rise and a sun set are two ends
of the checkerboard on which we play our game of life.
Or is it chess because it seems a bit more complicated?

Clouds appear to block our views.
We are often blind to what is happening out there.
We make a plan, a combination of hope and faith
in what we have to offer.

Small plans, big plans.
Some of us are content with what we see before us.
Others are driven to explore beyond what is in sight,
not content with where chance has placed them.

Some need to go beyond the limits,
to reach beyond apparent borders, challenge infinities.
Some of us insist on changing the game.
Some of us insist on playing our own game.

We were all little boys and girls in school,
playing the games that schooled us for our futures,
that rehearsed us for the roles we would play in life.
We were blank pages for our fates to be writ upon
but we practiced willy-nilly each scene of our lives
for a future we could not know.

What made one explore the farther reaches?
Who won the lottery, the swimming race
in your parent's private pool of genes?
Who lost the race for wealth and health?

Who was blessed with nurture generously invested?
Who had forbears' wealth to pave a golden road?
Who had the role model to follow for success or failure
and the determination to follow that road?
Who made his way regardless of circumstance?
Who was born in the wrong place at the wrong time?

Our futures blaze briefly against an eternal sky
like the minute flashing light of a dying star
vanishing into the infinite well of time.
Will someone remember our passage?
Are we a part of the Future?

ARE WE CLEAR ON THIS?

So we've lived a full life, careers and wives and kids
We're resting on our oars a bit, living on our savings,
doing the things we never had the time to do and thought
we might like to do, scratching itches we never had
the thought for, the mind for, the urge for.
Some of this stuff is fun, enjoyable, absorbing, so we could
take it seriously-or not. Maybe we're good enough
for a second career, or a third or fourth, but without the passion,
the hunger, the desperation to succeed.

The stakes are not that high. Our self-esteem is firmly planted
in our past accomplishments. But it's nice-nice to let the
    creativity
we have been suppressing flow out. If we make a mess of it
    so what?
Part of the fun is not really caring. No pressure, right!

But being what we are we can't help caring,
piling our ego on. We care alright! We want to
be really good at what we do.
It's hard for us to be any different than we always were.
We move more slowly but we still want to get there.

Can you stop wanting to change the world?
Can you stop caring about what seems to be an awful mess?
It only needs you to set it right?
Let's be clear on this-I can't stop caring.
Can you?
Why don't they ask us what we should do?
We still have all the answers.
Ask us!

THE ROLE OF THE PROPHET

In ancient times they were picked from the crowd-
the field was crowded-there were thousands over time,
the deluded, the demented, the diabolical,
seeking attention and a free lunch.

The true prophets, crying out they spoke for the be-all, the
    know-all,
the unknowable, with messages fashioned for the way
    people should behave
to avoid the catastrophes at alternative apogees.
Often they were those denying all the voices in their heads,
shrinking from the thankless task, seeking to shirk the
role thrust upon them by their inner natures,
seeking only the quiet corners, the existence of their silent
    lives.

Not for them the lonely place viewed by all the crowd,
    finding the words
from within themselves-the words expelled from their mouths-
to force minds to different paths, facing the hate, the rage
    of the chastised,
the outraged officialdom wrong-footed by an urgent
    condemnation
of the existing reality they had the tasks to administer.

With what fervor do we seek to avoid this role!

LIVIN' LIFE AS BEST I CAN

I'm livin' Life as best I can
don't really know the Why or When,
goin' onward rain or shine,
singin' you this song of mine.

had myself a kid or two,
found myself a lover true,
did some things to use my brain,
learned some things on living's train.
worry where the world is goin',
know it doesn't help to moan,
know it's better givin' than to take,
knowin' the human heart can break.

I'm livin' life the best I can
don't really know the Why or When,
goin' onward rain or shine,
singin' you this song of mine.

tellin' things you always knew,
the many things our lives can brew,
the sunny day that makes hopes rise,
the gentle touch, the sweet surprise,
disappointment often brings us low,
more to come than we can know,
we soldier on to see the comin' dawn,
in life's chess game, we are merely pawn.

I'm livin life the best I can,
don't really know the Why or When,

goin' onward rain or shine,
singin' you this song of mine..

I'm singin' songs to pass the time,
findin' words to fit my rhyme.
tellin' tales of Life I see,
findin' ways to set us free,
simple things that make life blessed,
leavin' behind the other rest,
hug us round and think good thoughts,
solve Life's puzzle-connect the dots.

I'm livin' Life as best I can,
don't really know the Why or When,
goin' onward rain or shine
singin' you this song of mine.

singin' you this song in rhyme,
singin' you this song of mine..

DID I TOUCH YOU?

My thoughts and the feelings I exude,
expressed from out my me
by the weight of all my living years
on my emotions-
did something you heard from me-
expressed from my tissues of lies and truths-
did some reflected light, did some glint of what I am
catch your ear, your eye, your heart, your mind?
Did I strike a chord – harmonic, dissonant,
fire a piercing flame of fear,
did an avalanche of insight arouse a symphony of feelings,
did I awaken an ache resonant of your experience?
Did I justify the message of my voice?
Did I justify the presence of my voice?
Did I justify my presence?
Did I touch you?

BLESSING FOR THE YEAR'S END

The year ends but time flows on
without man-made boundaries,
like liquid from the jar of Infinity.
Endless, suns rise and set.

Relevance springs to life
only in our minds
on this speck in the vastness of the universe.
What can we seek from this world?

A child smiles, or cries,
a mother turns to touch,
reaches out a hand in love.
We have a blessing for the year's end.

LONELY

Loneliness is corrosive,
acid-drip, eating, dissolving the sheaths of nerves
that allow us to resist, that keep us from curling up like
    autumn leaves
long parted from the tree of Life, the juice of Life.

We seek a caring eye, a touch, a tendril of compassion.
Straighten shoulders, walk on!
We would not miss it if we had not once bathed in its joy,
the joy of being cared for.

Walk on,
seeking a human's touch.

WEEPING

Emotions grip us, seize the heart, twist entrails,
unbidden, making tears flow,
soaring joy to burst the bonds that hold, so fierce,
our feelings in tight escrow,
searing pain we cannot contain,
unbearable hurt that we all must, willy-nilly, bear.
Find expression in a tear, reluctant or free,
the human condition, facing realized hope or deep despair.

Imagine, now, the gamut, what man's life-
and woman's too-its years do bring to us-
pride of accomplishment, dearly garnered
through years of strife and work, a plus.

Our losses, great and small, our errors irrevocable-
souls loved and lost beyond the earthly pale.
We regret at our leisure, recalling cruel memories,
each detail exquisitely painful mounted on living's scale.

Some seek with fortitude to suppress
and stifle the evidence of strong emotion's moist impress.
Stony face, harsh grimace, no outward vision
of the inner turmoil shielding deep distress.

Or simple smile, acquiesce, with coursing blood,
beating heart, unsteadily we stand
as rampant joy and exhilaration flare,
with harsh control we do the tears remand.

Potions course unseen through our inflamed vessels
unbidden prompting moistened eyes-
the pain of cruel scorning' sting,
suppressed are our swallowed hidden sighs.

Let fly our tears, emotions high, nerves tense,
we do well to cleanse, loose the pent up store,
they are corrosive far from vision's lens.
These deposits hidden, we know not how much more.

There may be poisons eating souls and bodies
that our ample tears could wash away.
Weep to relieve the buried tensions straining blindly
to find an outlet, pain or joy, that so much needs display.

Feel the raging beauty of release,
whether silent or painful keening,
with polite and gentle streams-surcease,
weeping yields relief, giving meaning

to the strong emotions inherent in our of human schemes.
I count it a blessing and a shelter, pain or joy, the force,
the motive for this uncontrolled issue of our seams,
this simple human act-instinctive in our human course.

Tears get us through the ups and downs of life bare intact,
easing the emotions at Life's essential core that we all face
    in fact.

LOOKING AROUND

We who have been here for a while,
now immersed in Life's events
we barely have the How to understand,
gratefully, if willy-nilly, surrendering our grasp
of change. We ask ourselves
what we have usefully to say.
Our young are impatient with us,
our attention wandering, missing some important details
they believe are crucial-we are slower to act
when they believe immediate action is urgent.

Well, what do we have to say?

People don't change that much.
Human motives have been the same
for all the centuries we have spent on this globe.
When we, the older, look around, can't we assess
human motivations more coolly, more rationally,
unmoved by the hue and cry of daily events.
Aren't we well placed to add something useful to the dialogue?

It's something to think about.

SHALL YOU SET YOUR WORLD ALIGHT?

The world is set alight before your eyes, effulgent inch by inch,
the orb of sun, rising slowly, slowly, the golden ray
creeping higher as if hauled up by a winch.
Then when we have spent the day,
tasking, fulfilling the needs our hopes evoke,
at end of day-it seems like a thunder's crack.
O! So swiftly the sun's light plunges down to black.
We contemplate Heaven's darkness falling on us like a cloak.

When we arise to meet that dawn, grey and then bright blue
so full of promise and potential blessings for our cause
we go forth striving, we have so very much to do,
dreaming at the end of our circle's well-earned applause.
Or if fortune be less smiling, our work one that will progress,
the hoped for rewards much delayed,
darkness falling, weary walking home, failures to confess,
only straining empty hands displayed.

Tomorrows yields for us potentialities so vast
we will summon courage to resume the fight.
We arise to face another fulsome day, energy amassed
as our night vanishes into the hours of brimming bright.
We daily gather strength to throw off our nightmare-filled
     dismay,
to organize and renew the dreams we have anew in sight,
to sally forth, like the courageous sun, no fear do we betray,
daily we go forth again prepared to set our world alight.

Coming Clean

Along a life of living how many hidden secrets
does our story hold,
some festering in our darkness,
twisting, turning, shaping our become?
Do we yet remember, wish forgotten,
memories deeply buried, frozen cold,
all the woundings scarring childhoods,
even manhood, knowing not the sum
of all the damages that are gathered
beneath apparent calm and tranquil mien,
oft hid from the conscious mind
but clearly shaping the people that we be?
Sometimes, suddenly surprising us,
we erupt in a violent explosive scene,
reactions far exceeding the circumstances
that roused emotions flying free.

Some will seek counsel to probe and investigate,
to lance the primal ache.
Most struggle on in silence,
perhaps shamed or confused by life's careen.
We wonder what possesses them, shadows them,
and places on their life a brake,
when the real prescription is
for all the dirty laundry to just come clean.

Some are fortunate to find a partner.
O! So rare! One who loves and really cares,
one with courage and persistence
to overcome defenses and beard the lion in its den;
one who can love, forgive the mean,

the petty shameful things fearing exposure-
dares to probe deep woundings, painful blamings
hidden from common human ken;
can evince from the partner the needed trust
to open these to the cleansing light of day
so that coming clean is possible,
salvaging a lov-ed soul
from a life that was in disarray.

RING DOWN THE CURTAIN

Ring down the curtain, the play has come to an end,
the story held our interest, we thought it might reveal a trend.
The beginning was a shocker, full of really exciting stuff,
the second act brought the changes, even though t'was
    really rough.

The final act was really one that was a record for the books-
who could believe how lives could alter and yield such
    joyous scenes-
we well know the fate we face, often little happy choice for
    us it brooks,
and yet the human spirit is dauntless, searching out the
    ways and means.

We learn again, whatever we face, remember that the play's
    the thing.
The world we face is made not just for chocolate truffle fun,
We have to pitch right in with all our might-the best we
    have to bring-
Then, O! Just maybe, then, we can clear the drear and give
    living life a run.

Ring down the curtain, strike up the band! Get the
    onlookers to stand!
The hero now comes out to bow, get his kudos from the
    respectful crowd.
He played his role as best he could, not perfect, but he still
    deserves a hand.
Let's hope the crowd will be so kind when he's laid out in a
    simple shroud.

We're all players in a drama; we each have a hero's starring
role,
we all take our turn to strut Life's stage, our piece to loud
and clearly say.
For us it rests to write the script, we each, like it or not,
must pay our toll,
the tough thing is to think through well just what it is the
role we'll play.

OUR TIME AND PLACE

Times were hard, there was no work, millions wandering
    place to place.
Lives, as through some evil quirk, were blasted from their
    ordered pace.

I was born, not knowing why, in a distant prairie town,
of parents wandered here to try to build a better life
than chance had their parents shown.
Seeming hostile, the world surround,
I could not know what was yet to come,
how peaceful and calm was this natal ground
compared with the places they came from.

I clearly remember, full of fear,
each day, as nightly at home we'd sit,
the news on the radio we would hear
of death and destruction in the world, large writ.

I could not know as conflict ceased,
that there was more horror to reveal
as news of death camps was released,
with an inhuman scale of evil we had now to deal.

How could one live with such a thought?
And yet we daily soldiered on.
For me, there is no way this stain to blot
but each day was daily built upon.

Hitler's horrors now to Stalin led,
there is no end to blood that's spilt,

the nuclear fear anew spread dread,
raised tensions all around, full tilt.

In spite of this for millions living was renewed,
Europe, Asia, brimmed with life anew,
as wiser men's sense was now accrued,
and better lives were sought not solely for the few.

China's complete horror story's not yet told,
in time it as well will all be seen,
teeming masses rise, of cultures old.
India's a place we've not yet been.

We do perceive there has been great gain
as millions labor and earn a place,
children prosper through parents' pain-
can we believe in God's good grace?

Through pain, Jews see their Promised Land
paid with their ravaged bodies, lives untold,
a place where, at last, they can proudly stand,
purchased with blood and sweat and gathered gold.

They've gained the right to stand on guard,
with brothers, watchful, at their backs,
shed softness, scruples, to be lean and hard,
awaiting so constant the many attacks.

New thoughts, new threats, yet do abound,
the world now is much electronified,
the world's fragile state proved in daily round,
no solutions evident, true and tried.

As while a child with my radio beside,
I wondered at the future that we would see.
Is there a miracle unseen that will turn the tide?
What can us from this constant fear set free?

My time, it now exceeds three score and ten,
many familiar faces vanished from the scene,
I wander where I will, only for the When
to set my limits, I am happily serene.

Yet, I ponder, ponder now my children's fate,
grandchildren too- I know I harbor hope
that they'll persist after I have cleaned my slate,
continue climbing onward, upward, life's demanding slope.

Come hold my hand, come warm my heart!
The life we live is just the start!
We have our unique Life-force to impart!
Let the life you live show the living art!

HER FACE THAT PREYS

She gazes round her world
from eyes so deeply lined,
the tracks of pain inflicted,
incised and well defined,
carved deep in flesh of others
as she, like a reigning bird of prey,
her smiling mouth a rictus, stands,
stylish bobbed hair here on display.

She disgorges acid wit and wisdom,
for watchers gathered round,
that pierce and wound wherever they land,
seeking out, as they are found,
the most vulnerable for her pleasantries,
fingers, claw-like, sharp like pins,
damaged lives, rivulets of pain
flow free from the web of images she spins.

Too often, here among us
like a queen bee from her nest,
she spreads her honeyed poison round her
wounding all, each life she does infest.
With guile or guilt or golden ropes
she reels her victims close,
gazing innocently round her, sweetly smiling
she delivers the searing dose.

It is delivered so off-handedly
the victim is oft struck dumb,
reeling, wounded and in pain,
it is dispensed with such aplomb.

She is offended, often angry,
that victims sometimes take amiss
remarks "so well intended", why
should they lead to such distress?

Wherefrom is born this bile
distilled in a female breast,
how were formed these creatures of our clay,
our humanity to test.

Wherefrom this corrosive bent nurtured in their past?
How was learned this evil skill,
or was this just a random genetic cast
that created this genius malign will?

We know them here among us,
we flee them far whenever we can
seeking shelter through our distance,
from that cruel glance that miles can span.

Deliverance will come only, surely,
when time has dulled that steely gaze
and healing death has stilled that tongue
and brought that face to an end of days.

INTERLUDE

In the company of strangers
I make polite faces,
shielding thoughts in the mangers
of my mind. Paces,
measuring my step to ensure I'm staying in the group,
hiding myself under a secret canopy, no separation from the
    troupe.

We all find ourselves in places where we do the politics,
we march closely in the group's traces, playing all the tricks.
We surrender not our souls, hiding our persona close inside,
paying all the tolls for pleasing, careful always then to hide
the realities we are. We can then belong,
following others' rules afar, yet ourselves continue strong.

We have our times when the rules that rule are ours.
We, then, forceful, make the laws,
the group we lead feeds on our powers,
inclining to our leadership cause,
and we carry onward in full flower,
the essence that we are, the focus, first of all, the peer,
leading beyond the bar, to the hiding persons like a seer.
As we do when others lead, we must needs be the Whos
    who wisdom wreak,
to tap riches we then need, the task's goal assured from
    prospects bleak.
The rich secret in our group resides,
the perfect answers we do seek,
to find those answers sole our group confides.

For all of us, sometimes life intrudes.
We all must live our interludes.

CIRCLE OF FRIENDS

Wrought in clay, gathered are a group of friends,
I wrote a verse with sentiment sufficient to my ends,
I celebrate the wonder and the magic, the messages it sends
for those of us belonging to this precious circle of our friends.

We strive alone, each man his private path attends,
destinies diverse, the unseeing hand of fate descends,
yet, through it all, a healing balm to us it lends,
knowing that we belong to a circle of warm loving friends.

Our grouping has many random elements which it blends,
blundering sometimes, friends are open to amends,
generosity and warmth is the message that it sends,
we cling to this membership circle of our closest friends.

As the years roll on we know not what the future for us
    portends,
we all face unknowns, against all the cautious mind defends,
it yields us great solace-though we are strong none of us
    pretends
we are not grateful for that unique circle of our faithful friends.

V

m

COMING TO TERMS

CYCLE

Beginning's pains beyond imagining as parents build for
  hoped-for goals,
that children, shielded danger, might realize precious
  product of their toils,
we, offspring, gave no thought, or little, to our parent's
  careful oversight,
accepting all as due, travail, treasure, thoughtless-all our
  very own by right.

We in turn launch dynastic issue, afloat, or sinking, the
  rushing tide of life,
watched, as did our parents, helpless, joyful passing-passage
  full of strife?
Did we think on it, our parent's suffering, as we view our
  children's course,
engaging all Life's sea of troubles, inherent part-essential, of
  living's force.

Surviving through it all and reaching, finally, an ending
  living-place serene,
viewing past woundings, sore, can we hope for them a more
  fulfilling scene?
And what of grandkids, when we've shuffled-weary-off this
  "mortal coil",
will we retain across the passage, visions, the happenings on
  this roiling soil?

Content me now to bless my current joy. I hopeful wishes
  my children send,
life cycle proceeding, more resembles mine when it comes
  finally to the end.

THE LAST TIME I SAW MY FATHER

Driving away, angry, staring out the car window at my Dad.
I had traveled far from struggling home-based student
to be an independent man with wife and child and my way
    to make.
Focus, focus, focus, education to complete, to gain a career
    ascendant,
public speeches, television interviews, newspaper coverage,
travel to the great cities of the east, travel far and wide
around the globe and no visits home- I was obsessed with
    pride.

"You are welcome to my home," my father had to me said,
"and bring my grandson, but don't bring her here around"
I took it all in stride.

Choose between wife and parents? No question of my choice!
Blind loyalty was to my new family.
I did not speak to him again until the day he died.

Perhaps they knew her in a way I did not?
Did she show open disrespect?
Did she show them she did not love their son?
Did she show them what took me more than a decade to decide?

I remember my father at the kitchen table,
hired to shovel coal, with no formal education-
for almost five years struggling and mastering
the mysteries of steam engineering and refrigeration
to build a professional career-
filling me with an offspring's pride.

My father struggled to build a life for his family-
to build a life for me.
I weep. Unforgivable! My obsessive pride !

I never had that conversation with my father
about my admiration for him.
I never thanked my father for my life before he died.

AN IMAGE OF AFRICA

A generation has come and gone, but the images linger
in the deeper crevices of my mind.

Chaotic streams of humanity, filling the rutted bi-ways
where roads we know have never gone.
Beasts of burden called women, a child, or two, on the
    backside,
carrying the stuff of life.
Firewood, water, containers with unknown contents,
bales of cloth,
machinery of unknown origin or destination.

And the colors- oranges, yellows, blues, all of variegated hue,
a cacophony of color, sounds and motion in the
    marketplace.

Products of every description,
on rickety table,
on dusty floor,
on a scrap of cardboard,
on a piece of cloth.

Venture into the slaughterhouse
where meats and fish
are displayed with all their charms,
to the humming accompaniment
of the sounds and sights of flying fauna.

Children wander everywhere
offering objects of every description,
begging, with soulful, searching, eyes,

seeking a spark of compassion,
seeking an advantage.

Show mercy
and face an inundation by a mass of people
pleading the urgency of their desperation.

The great palaces of former white occupation are
empty of their owners,
windows and doors long gone,
teeming with humanity
huddling around family campfires in disused living rooms
devoid of gracious furniture,
long-burned to ward of chill, to cook a meal.

Young women, very young,
and much older,
trolled ceaselessly for means of sustenance,
offering what it was they had to give
that would earn them the means to live another day.

I traveled these scenes,
eating-I thought-so bravely-
the foods offered in the streets.
I was learning
how fortunate I was
to have been born in another place.

Exiled to the grand hotels and their fine restaurants
with hired chance companions,
I was paid handsomely with foreign treasure
to no effect on the ills I had come to cure.
I knew I walked among many of the soon-to-be dead.

FINDING MY VOICE

Reach, reach, reaching out, I am reaching out,
I can almost touch it, almost touch it,
the point I wish to touch if I can, stretching-
if I can touch it will I have found my place- found my voice?
Will I have reached the point I wish to reach-need to reach-
to communicate what I need to say-must say-
so you can understand what it is I need to say
if I am to witness that I have found my voice.
Is this what I live to do?
Can you hear it, can you bear it?
Can you bear what it is I need to say?

Our world is in danger, do you see the danger?
Can you, do you believe the danger?
Will you act to save it-
the world-will it act?
All of you, will you act to save it?
Can you hear me, do you hear my voice?

Have I found my voice in vain?

MAKING OF MORE, MUCH LESS

City of Kisangani,
its palaces in ruins;
its wide streets rubbled with excess,
its owners, its inheritors,
they know not what they possess,
they are indifferent to the jungle's march,
of the city in distress;
they endeavor it seems, even daily,
to make the more they have, much less.

The stifling heat of the ancient decaying inland port,
one thousand miles from the distant Afric' coast,
on the mighty Niger, many nations it does sort,
called the Zaire River by our tyrannical Congo host.

I sojourn in the city in a suite in the Hotel Grand.
I come to give assistance and to this land to extend a hand.
Mayhap I will restore an enterprise to employment here
    expand,
finding the means to build a future for this rich distress-ed
    land.

Once an Afric' glory of imperial Belgium's crown,
the jungle's ample riches, its soil with copper brown,
gold, diamonds, slaves, all of them shipped down
on ships, vast barges, towed to the capital town.

My hours are long and difficult; the discussions are deep
    and broad.
The work goes very slowly as each tortuous step we plod.

The ruins mask the beauty where the white man's foot has
    trod.
Despite our every effort, what we seem to build is yet a fraud.

I hide each evening in my suite, seeking surcease from my
    mental pain.
I walk in Kisangani, search for and find a woman in the rain.
"Come home with me," I say and very soon with me she's lain.
Her company the whole night long I surely did not disdain.

I welcomed her attentions, I was most surely grateful I confess.
I awakened, at first light to see her crying there in deep distress,
"What's the matter?" asked I in fright, gently hurrying my
    caress,
"My breasts!" She wailed. "How can I make the more of
    them much less?"

RESCUE

Inconsequential, attendance at a family affair.
This woman brought her teen-aged child, newly into puberty,
new-found breasts pushing shape into her blouse.
Her mind, more child-like,
the impulsiveness of three, or maybe ten,
this child, rescued
from the horrors of Ceaucesceau's Romania.
Babies, in orphanages without nurture,
without food or care,
a Mengelean experiment on those who did not die,
for those who lived for years without a human's touch.

This beautiful face, this woman-child,
with her fifty-year-old mother
whose husband fled the rigors of the task.
Who will shelter this woman-child
when the mother is seventy, or more?
Who will rescue the mother?

TENDER, MY APOLOGIES

Imagine all the things I've done and not done,
hurt and pain as residues, slime left in my snail's pace,
shining iridescence in the lowering light of my passage
stretching back, lo, these many years.

Can one pass through this life without doing damage?

Looking back, were not the worst the things undone,
unsaid, unthought, as I went careening onward
intent on goals-look neither to the right or left?
Focus, focus, focus- that's the thing!

Those attendant on our passage, muted by wonder
at our positive aspiration, utter not a word, not a sound.
They silently speak!

"See me! What about me? I need your attention
focused on me! I am a tender shoot sprung from your branch,
your sapling tree, trampled underfoot by your passage.
I was at your side; did you not see my needs-
my need for answers I had to seek elsewhere?"

Were there others who would have flowered,
harboring precious seeds, needing the reflected
sunshine of my bright attention, that failed to germinate,
lying fallow so long the energy of Life abandoned them?

Were there some that did blossom
from the warmth of my random glance?

Did my force of nature leave unflowered blossom buds
in my wake, struck inert and lifeless by my shade?

Is this the debt I owed my time for the gifts of nature,
the sparks of untutored initiative that spurred me
on to the trails I blazed in the formless landscape
we all face in mapping each our way?

Need I tender my apologies for the unseen wounds,
the scars, the damages inherent in the heedless passage
which was my life?

SKYWARD

Flying above Arizona to a Houston destination,
leaving my bride behind,
on my way to Panama.
Flying my baby computer for the first time,
I feel like a master of the universe
with the dynamism of America at my feet,
spanning the continent,
seeking control of the powers of the cosmos.

I live in the year 2011,
a different existence from my origins seven decades ago.
Today, though we live on earth as we did then,
we also occupy the clouds.
Who can imagine the future?
Who can imagine where the future will fly us?

When my grandchildren look at their past
will they have rescued this planet from our excess?
Will their lives be more fulfilling?
Can America-can the world, find the answers?

I progress skyward to join the community of living essence,
to take my place in the continuum-
can it become too crowded as we add more souls.
Will we take too much space when we are
seventy billion instead of seven?

Do souls take space?
Is our essence sub-divided to accommodate
new numbers, as places have been made
for my grandchildren in the community of the living?

Where do we find space for insects that also live?
And bacteria?
Do they not count? Are they not sentient?
Do we become crowded in our infinities,
counting life in other universal hideaways?

My body is circling the world.
My mind is circling the cosmos
My mind flies skyward with my soul,
but my heart remains in Arizona with my lover.

WHISPERING THOUGHTS-
THE GOOD TIMES

They are in my head, tumbling through all
the debris of stuff stored over near eighty years.
I thought I might make sense of it sometime,
but more just gets piled on top of everything else.
I lose my place and just throw up my hands.

I know there is stuff there that bears a look.
When I think about all the growing up,
being scared all the time and afraid people
would know I was afraid.

They must have known I was frightened,
all those immigrant kids who wanted to fight with me.
I would just have to fight them,
rolling around on the ground, I would have to fight them,
because there was nothing else to do even though I was afraid.

My fists felt like powder puffs
but some of them bled.
Afterward they stopped wanting to fight
and wanted to be friends.
But I still hated them because I was still afraid.

I remember when Harry ran over to hit me
and my sister stood in front of me
and she said "don't you touch my brother"
and he didn't.

I remember fighting Mikey
I remember fighting Danny.
I remember fighting Tony, his brother.
I remember being hit in the head with a stone thrown by Billy.
I remember Stan poked me in the ribs with his elbow.
I felt it for a week.

I remember Ed picked a fight with me in Junior High School
When I came out the door after classes-
there was a whole crowd waiting
because Ed had told everyone there was going to be a fight.
I didn't want to fight but there was no choice
so I hit him as hard as I could in the face.
His nose started to bleed.
I held out my hand, saying "first blood".
I don't remember what happened after that.
I did not even see the blow,
but when I woke up I was alone on the ground.
The whole crowd had gone and left me for dead.

Tony and Ed died long ago
and I'm glad
because all my life I've been afraid
that I would have to fight them again.

I was afraid because my Dad was afraid.
We all knew it was there. It was about being poor,
but we didn't know what it was all about.
So we were afraid, too
No job for all those years and the family on welfare.

I didn't feel bad about that because I didn't know what it was.
I thought everybody lived like that.

But everyplace we moved to was a worse place than the last.
So now I know why my Dad was afraid,
why he went ballistic when I lost a glove or a cap
'cause you gotta' have those things in the Canadian winter
and there was no money.

So I felt poor. I never realized that I should feel bad
about being poor, but I was always conscious
growing up about how many of my friends were not poor,
with fathers a doctor, or a dentist, or a lawyer,
or they had a grocery-my cousin's father had a grocery.

My clothes weren't the best but I never thought
about that until I became aware of girls.
Then it was always in the back of my mind,
so it must have affected my self-confidence.

When my Dad finally got a job as the War began,
Mom saved up for a down payment for a house
in a decent neighborhood.
When we moved I knew my life had changed forever.
But the feeling of being poor never went away.

My Dad was always trying to get people to like him-
not us-other people.
It hurt me because I knew it would never work.
Why weren't we first on his list?
He would do them favors and give them little gifts
but it never got him the respect and approval
he was looking for.

His own father left him behind when he came to Canada
to make his fortune. My Dad came to Canada

after his mother died of typhus when he was twelve.
He lived traveling between relatives for a few years
with his little brother until his father sent him money
to bring his cousin to Canada to be a wife for him.
He got as far as London, and then had to run and hide.
They wanted to send him back because he got Pink Eye.

After he came to Canada and married and had children
the cousin who married his father wouldn't let him come
to his father's house because she didn't want
his children's competition with the grandfather
affecting attention for her own kids.
He was still an orphan.

His lack of education didn't stop him
from becoming a stationery engineer.
He got a chance because all the young men had gone to war.
I remember him studying at the kitchen table
every night after work
for years. But, still, he was always trying
to get strangers to like him
and he was always afraid of the Depression.

I always wanted to be independent.
I wouldn't let anybody help me,
leaving home as early as I could
I never wanted to be dependant on anyone.

When I grew up I had an argument with my Dad.
I didn't talk to him for twenty-five years before he died.

So I had wives and kids,
and I threw myself into my education
and every job I had with everything I had.
I didn't try to curry favor
like my Dad but worked at the studying and the job.
I sought approval only for the excellence of my work
That came before everything so I could succeed.
That was so even if it meant I wasn't really available
a lot of the time to those who were close to me.

Isn't that's almost the same thing as what my Dad did?

Thank heavens I remember some really good weekends with
   the kids
when they were growing up. I cling to that.

I wish I had said goodbye to my Dad and thanked him.

Maybe others could learn from me about all this.

THE ORANGE TREE

Imagine,
I have an orange tree-
all mine.

I come from the frozen North
where three months of summer is a blessing,
and plant growth is fast and furious,

then, mostly, it dies, to be replanted in the Spring.
No fruit trees there except in a few places,
a few very fortunate places.

We have trees that eke out growth-slowly, very slowly-
and grow some, but no, mostly no fruit trees-or at least no
    orange trees.

So here I am in Arizona,
and I have an orange tree,
and, get this, it gives two crops a year,
and sweet, sweet as nectar are my navel oranges.
and I don't even water them!

And when the crop is in
each day I can pick a handful, and eat them.
I have a whole tree and I never run out-
except it's a race between me and the birds-
who will eat the most.

This boy from the frozen North
has his own orange tree.
Today, I am smelling orange blossoms.

Yippee! The orange tree is blossoming.

ACHE GROUP

Our best times have gone marching on,
leaving me as a sentinel-
draping creeping skin with warm fabric.
O how good it feels to warm our bones!

We witness onrushing change, pell mell;
though some remain in the thick of things.
Most are gathered, streamed, channeled
into many a fine edifice,

"Everything you need, really!
I know you'll be happy here
with your own age group!"
Tucked away.
out of the way.
not getting in the way.

"We'll visit you every week,
if not more often,
certainly, more often."

Why do we smile at the lies when we
know we don't believe them.
Maybe because we need to believe.

Why would we want to be
with our own age group?
Our own ache group?
To share our pain?
Our symptoms?

Our winding down the path?
And to see you, …maybe?

Surround me with the young!
Challenge me to match their stride,
their wits,
their life.

Let me struggle on
until I know no longer that I care.

BUILDING BLOCKS

Looking back,
I think to see the seamless see-saw
of the ocean of my past.
But it is not so.
If I think about it, my history is more
like the "scape" of a giant city,
full of highs and lows.

Think about it!
Use the perspective of your bygone years
to give yourself the gift
of second sight.

There were building blocks we put
together in our early lives,
piece by piece,
as we put in place the skills of living, surviving-
talking, walking-
learning to read the alphabet,
learning to read the faces around us-
questioning-are they friend or foe,
help or hindrance-
counting on our toes and fingers
the things we had to do
to draw close those we valued
and defend against those we had to fear-
learning the skills we would need to trade
for the things we would learn to want.

Lots of building blocks went into
building the first home we placed on our life map.

There were the many ups and downs.
as we sought to build the skyscrapers of our attainment,
the more we had at risk, the more we dared
and the more we had to lose.
Who can boast a life building only straight up?

All of us have had our "sloughs of despond"-
in career, financial reverse, health or family events,
finding/losing a love, a child, a parent-
overreaching pride, the blindness of arrogance,
plain stupidity, carelessness, blind circumstance.

Look back and see the highs and lows!
Did we let it defeat us or did we re-assemble
our building blocks and build anew?
Did we survive to appreciate that time
when what we often crave, having reached safe harbor,
is the seamless see-saw of a peaceful ocean for our lives from
which we could contemplate the distant heights of the past,
happy, O so happy to be where we are?

Now, our building blocks have been given
to our children to play with.

THE INEFFABLE BEAUTY OF THE NOW

This instant we share a touch, a smile, the incomparable joy
    of the Now!

No matter how many years have swept across the bar of life,
no matter that unknowns may sunder our living time like a
    knife
no matter how painful every trial that we have faced,
woven into time's fabric, in our minds indelibly interlaced,
treasured memories in our nurtured consciousness we guard,
retaining of the fragments of our past life a precious shard.

Some have lived through horrors that wreak havoc on the
    mind,
cruelty so bestial it beggars the imagination to recall-
the partners who shared their pain and joy left many years
    behind.
Those memories brim their hearts-tears unbidden fall.

They relive another time. They recall now the beauty of that
    Then,
rare moments that the world was perfect, now yearning for
    a When-
that life could bless them then with a rare repeat
of that instant when their life was so fully then replete

Teetering on the edge of ecstasy, the very brow,
they little knew it was for them the single Now,
notwithstanding their later years of pain, bitter defeat,
that single moment was the one that made their life complete.

Guard you well! Our existence-our passage-flashes by
O so quick. Lives awash, flooded-distractions catch the eye,
on every frantic side, our attentions wander as through a
   magic trick,
The issues seem compelling as our lives are built, brick on
   brick.

But are they the essential things to which we wish all our
   lives to confide?
Pay attention to what does matter, be careful what it is that
   you decide
Contemplate the course of life, as you your golden moments
   freely spend-
consider well the focus where you do your prime attention
   lend?

Consider well the What, the When, the Why, above all, the
   How
Be sure you do not, careless, miss, the ineffable beauty of
   the Now.

CAN YOU SEE ME?

Can you see me through your eyes?
How do I seem?
Was I bright and bushy-tailed?
Did I tell a joke?

You came to see me because I was such fun,
always something interesting to say,
challenging you, leaving something in your mind,
quicksilver thoughts to slide swiftly into the thirsty spots
needing irrigation for growth in kind.
Maybe now you can entertain your friends.
Our visits always have for us such good ends.

Not today!
Today I am vanishing into myself,
down my own rabbit hole.
I am vanishing into myself searching for my Me.
Come back tomorrow
if you wish to see what I have become.

ALONE

We sit in groups to shelter ourselves from the loneliness we feel.
We warm ourselves by rubbing shoulders with a few
whose company can still the inner sadness
for a while, those who can distract us from
the loneliness that lies at the heart of being human.

We live our lives eternally alone like a single tree standing
in the forest surrounded by companions.
Rarely we find someone who can persuade us
that two can be one,
but in the end we all die alone.

ON PARADE

What shall we do? What shall we do?
Up and down, we swing around!
Whatever happened to slow and steady wins the race?
With the turmoil whirling around us it is hard to think clearly.
What to do, what to say, where to go. Stop! Just stop!

I am past the time when I should be worrying about this,
but I am in the midst of the worst convulsion
in economic affairs in our lifetime.
Easy to say, why me?
We always try to resist saying that even if we feel like that.

Why should I have to live through "interesting times"?
I suspect anytime we face these situations, for us,
times are much "too interesting" for our taste.
Like it or not, it's up to me
to make lemonade from my lemons.

Gee! I hate it when it rains on my parade!

MY LIFE'S DESSERT

So it goes! The wheel of life, now up, now down-
do we know where we are at now?
Is this our high point?

Will we look back
with the perspective of passing years
to know that this was our best time
at life's banquet
and we lacked only the relish
of joy and appreciation
to add the ultimate spice?

Or, that the black shade
that we then deemed so dire and dark
was but a way station on the path of horrors
we had yet to face-
the tyranny of a misbegotten fate?

How not to fear the future
in a life so crowned with joys?
I look around at my world,
the colorful coulee of Life's dessert
soaking into the greedy textures of my being.
The full portion I have consumed on my plate,
the sweet juices on my tongue,
have flushed away the bitter aftertaste
of some early courses.

Have my life's goodies been stuffed with cream
skimmed from the lifetimes
of a million others less fortunate?

How will this repast reach its conclusion?
Has the Chef prepared a surprise for us
for when, replete with years, we push back
from the table set with life's banquet
to join the throng milling about on the promenade
for the infinite period of existence's digestion?

SHARDS OF A LIFE LIVED

Delving into lives archeologic, sifting layers of ash,
a careful examination of living life's trash,
find a bone, a kernel of grain,
stone worked to make a point,
coins corroded to a stain
ceramic shards, images joint
telling teased elaborate tales
as to whether a civilization succeeds or fails.

Search a dwelling for a life's recent passing,
see inanimate objects, their role in life unknown,
many images are strangers digitally amassing,
assessing what threads in a previous life were sown.

Here, now I write
in words quite clear,
of the product, neuronic,
my electric charge a smear,
coursing, metastatic, hormonic,
abounding with chemical cheer,
celebrating a life lived at the fullest-
yes, lived large, aspiring to be a seer.

These are then the shards I leave-life crashing-
will they convey the complex truth of what I was?
Or, will they launch diverse theories re my life-full dashing-
of struggles-conflicts-all things sacrificed for a precious cause?

Here now are the bare bones of the life I many decades lived-
I aspired, in life to make a small, worthy, yet indelible mark-
from all this, all my doings-these shards can perhaps be sieved-
in the lives that I have touched, I brought some light in
    from the dark.

FORGET TOMORROW

I am looking to my tomorrows,
I know not yet what there I'll find-
Yesterday, it had its sorrows,
my Todays to me are much more kind.

Each life is balanced on a knife-edge,
good or bad, it's full of care,
we bleed, mayhap apply a bandage,
we take it on then whatever we find.

Harbingers we see abounding,
grit your teeth and gird your loins,
count your joys, some random wishes
yielded from fluid Trevi's coins.

Let me treasure all the joys
that briefly burnished my living's space,
Future pain our joy alloys,
our blind Tomorrows we must yet face.

We soldier on for good or ill,
with life-lease comes no guarantee,
we embrace whatever Fate does will-
joys we earn do not come free.

Memory dwells on the sunny day-
special times when the bright was clear-
now, forget tomorrow, dance and play,
happily embrace our presence here.

SITTING IN THE SUN

All my life I've rushed around
too busy to just sit,
so many things to do here on the ground,
scrabbling like an ant to fit
in all the things just must be done
to hold up my living's end-
all the important places I must run
all the right messages to send.

Now I'm sitting in the sun
admiring, sailing free, the scudding clouds,
leaves turning their brilliant colors dun,
enjoying passing faces in the crowds.
I feel the evening chill, winter coming
that I used to dread-daily-work in the arctic cold-
soon we travel elsewhere for our sunning,
to where heat turns the drying green to gold.

I once pondered what would be,
if ever I could shed the toiler's load,
whether I would survive, escape to see
a quieter time on living's road.
I burned to work, it was my pride,
I could not imagine a life without
a tough job to do, sought no free ride,
measuring up, the group's "good scout".

We never dreamed we could just sit,
twiddle thumbs-just passing time-

full agenda-pouring tea; crochet and knit-
writing verses and perfecting rhyme.

Here it is! The latest news!
Pleasure flourishing in the setting sun,
gathering round my offspring crews,
amusing me as my idle times are run.

NIGHTLIGHTS

Do we see better in the dark?
I am sitting here at three o'clock in the morning.
I have been roused by the aches
and pains of growing old.
The arthritis is getting to me.

A few months ago I was basking in the heat,
the intensely dry heat of Arizona.
I was exercising every day, vigorously,
perhaps too vigorously for a seventy-seven year old.
I felt great, great to be in full command of all my limbs,
jumping-running when I felt like it-
sweating profusely from my vigorous efforts.

I went to Mexico and in full sight of the sparkling Pacific,
in the dry heat at the tip of the Baja, in California Sur,
I did more of the same, throwing my limbs in every direction.
I worked on my flexibility-never my strong point-
I felt like a Greek God.

Then a long trip to my European home,
cramped economy seating in a crowded plane.
Awaking the next morning I could hardly get out of bed.
All my joints hurt. I couldn't lift my arms without acute pain.
I couldn't lift my legs to put on my socks
for the pain in my knees and hips.

Suddenly I was all my years.
I asked myself, is this the way life will be for me
from now on.....on and on.....forever?
What happened to age me so suddenly?

The X-rays say deteriorating joints.
The physiotherapist says galloping arthritis.
Could the villain be Irish dampness, the "soft" days I love?

The son-in-law, a former doctor,
says massive doses of anti-inflammatories are needed
to get the swelling down from overuse of the joints.
I clung to the remedy with the hope
that it would lead to quick relief.
The regular GP asked what I would do
when the anti-inflammatories cease to work,
as they do.
The acupuncturist said I had stagnant chi.
The physiotherapist gave me painful exercise.
When he increased mobility with the pain,
he doubled the exercise.
He promised I would find these less painful than
when he began to manually exercise my limbs,
which he never did.
He promised me I would never regain my full mobility,
so get used to it.

I saw progress in the hips
which I ascribed to the acupuncturist.
I needed painkillers for the shoulders
which I ascribed to the physiotherapist
My world became circumscribed
by my limited capacity to absorb and
overlook the pain of movement in everyday life.
Now I feel my hips, my elbows and my shoulders
that once fully functioned without any awareness of their
    existence.
My bubble has been burst.

I am consoled now that I will get better.
I know now that things will never be
as good as they were before.
I am now through middle age.
I am older.
I see my future in the brightness of nightlights
piercing the mists of my illusions
that I can go on feeling forever young.

It would be good to go back a few months
to that time of illusion when I basked
in the feeling that my body was wholly at my command.
I had gotten used to all the precautionary pills
that kept my insides feeling and working as they should.
Now I am in a different phase, a different place, a different space.
I see darker days ahead.

We must think this through.
We know now how some can contemplate
the final sleep as a laying down of burdens,
as a release, as a blessing.

We who are so full of appreciation
of the joys of living, the blossoming flower,
the incredible symmetry of each petal
in every imagined hue; the burbling brook,
the light dancing through flights of fancy on its surface,
the touch of silken skin-feel it under your fingertips-
and in the aches of your memory-
the warm embrace that banishes hurt and gloom,
a child's laugh that brightens every darkness;
the well-spiced meal that whispers
the love contained in its preparation;

the tart-sweet delight of apple pie
enrobed in a short and crumbly crust
that echoes the wonder of creation;
the sunburst through cloud
that re-invents a world an instant sooner dark,
the mist-like rain on a grateful cheek,
the well-turned phrase that gives pause
and insight into the heart of existence;
the heart-break thought that brings on tears,
the vista, a grand and glorious hymn to God;
the tiny insect struggling to make its tortuous way-
we glory in all this.

How I weep when, surrounded by my brethren,
I read that the truth shall go forth from Jerusalem
and I see it happen every day;
I am astounded by the myriad things that confound
enumeration, description or even conception,
like the cosmos beyond our hope of view.

We conceive and understand growth and new life
But we recognize as well a longing for surcease.
Pain beyond control or hope of cessation
that can bring us to this desperate state,
a willing surrender of the state of life.

But let me regale me again with some of the joys
I would have to leave behind,
perhaps to persuade me there is more here
worth the bearing of all pain.

See/taste the yellow yolk of a poached egg
raining over multigrain buttered toast

with sliced juicy tomatoes rampant,
sprinkled just enough with kosher salt.
Witness a slab of garlic salami
on a large crust of rye bread from Winnipeg,
not too fresh, with perhaps a touch of hot mustard.
Remember Mrs.Whyte's cured herring with onions,
knockwurst and chips with ketchup, Heinz of course,
veal shoulder chops, beaten thin,
dipped in egg, rolled in bread crumbs,
fried until crisp in an open skillet;
the soup my honey makes from just about anything
with a little cayenne and a toasted buttered baguette;
spaghetti bolognaise made just right by Italians
so the spaghetti is al dente
and the tomato sauce, thick, red, and caramelized;
fried onions of almost any description;
Dublin's Leo Burdock battered codfish and chips
with salt, vinegar and ketchup;
France's buttered baguette and marmalade
with strong sugared coffee and cream in a sunny cafe;
full sour pickles made with dill and only brine;
Schwartz's Montreal rib steak, grilled medium rare;
apple pie in some long-lost New Brunswick village café,
hot chocolate in a Tuscany hideaway;
Cologne beer in a flute;
Carlsberg ale in a noisy Dublin Pub, no Guinness for me,
Lindys cheesecake in New York-none of this airy stuff,
special Burgundy wine in Pouligny-Montrachet,
allio and olio spaghetti in any Italian restaurant
where it is made by Italians,
grilled lamb chops at Chez Max in Loro Ciufena, Tuscany,
....the list goes on, and that is just the food.

Did I tell you about all the melodies I love?
The list is too long.

I can describe the glories of the mind
expressed in the buildings on New York's Fifty-second Avenue,
those on Chicago's loop,
the internal hanging balconies in Atlanta,
some of the jewels in Phoenix and San Francisco,
the pomp and majesty of downtown London,
the eternal beauty of Paris,
the adventure of the new Tel Aviv
and the pink blossoming of Jerusalem,
the beach towers of Miami.
What of the places I have never seen
like the Taj Mahal and the Alhambra,
the curiosities of Dubai?

What of the written word?
I am consumed by the genius of Shakespeare,
and the other giants of the English language.
Shall I surrender the thundering prophets
of my own heritage-
the historic writings of the Hebrews?
What of the perplexities of Job?
What of the wise of the Indian sub-continent
and the Chinese?

I have yet a moment or two before my husk
is so dry there is no translation can be made
from the messages on the rods and cones of my retinas.

If I keep this up I shall want to linger here forever.

I think I shall remain here
as long as the warm hand of my bride
clings to mine and damn the pain!

I will rest here until the nightlights fade.